T0356194

Praise for Kwame Alexander

"Kwame Alexander seems to have an almost hypnotic command over audiences, whether he's speaking to squirmy first graders, high school seniors, or a room full of publishing executives."

—*New York Times*

"In helping his readers redefine their place in the world, Kwame Alexander is nurturing the next generation of leaders."

—*Oprah Daily*

"With radiance and poetic precision, Kwame Alexander's words will remind you of art's infinite sustenance."

—Adrienne Brodeur, author of bestselling memoir *Wild Game: My Mother, Her Lover, and Me* and executive director of Aspen Words

"I've seen Kwame Alexander motivate ninth graders and teachers, librarians and corporate executives. He has this poetic way of reinforcing the importance of believing in ourselves, taking risks, and following our dreams . . . I can't think of a better person to share and spread that message to others than Kwame Alexander."

—Matt Follett, president of Follett USA

"His ability to authentically relate to his readers is a skill around which he has built his career. Kwame is beloved by parents, educators, and students for his ability to ignite a love of reading, but his impact extends beyond just an introduction to books: He also opens the door for readers to explore their own emotional depths."

—Jordan Lloyd Bookey, co-founder and host of *The Reading Culture Podcast*

Say Yes

Other Books by Kwame Alexander

How Sweet the Sound: A Soundtrack for America

Why Fathers Cry at Night: A Memoir in Love Poems, Letters, Recipes, and Remembrances

The Door of No Return series

The Undefeated

Becoming Muhammad Ali (with James Patterson)

Kwame Alexander's Free Write: A Poetry Notebook

Light for the World to See: A Thousand Words on Race and Hope

The Write Thing

The Playbook: 52 Rules to Aim, Shoot, and Score in This Game Called Life

The Crossover

Acoustic Rooster and His Barnyard Band

KWAME ALEXANDER

Say Yes

Find Your Passion, Unleash Your Potential,
Transform Your Life!

Andrews McMeel
PUBLISHING®

Andrews McMeel Publishing
a division of Andrews McMeel Universal
1130 Walnut Street, Kansas City, Missouri 64106

www.andrewsmcmeel.com

In partnership with Mango Publishing Group, Inc.
5966 S. Dixie Hwy, Suite 300, South Miami, FL 33143
and
Big Sea Entertainment

Cover, layout, and design: Roberto Núñez
Author photo: Rowan Daly

ISBN: 978-1-5248-9982-0
Library of Congress Control Number: On file

ATTENTION: SCHOOLS AND BUSINESSES
Andrews McMeel books are available at quantity discounts with bulk
purchase for educational, business, or sales promotional use. For
information, please email the Andrews McMeel Publishing Special Sales
Department: sales@andrewsmcmeel.com.

For Nikki Giovanni, who taught me to always do things, even without guarantee, especially without guarantee, because that's what's got to happen, because saying YES to yourself is the only way you get to decide what matters, what's right, and what's good . . . enough.

You may encounter many defeats, but you must not be defeated. In fact, it may be necessary to encounter the defeats, so you can know who you are, what you can rise from, how you can still come out of it.

—Maya Angelou

Prologue

In 2024, I was asked to give the commencement speech at the American University School of Communication and School of Education graduation ceremony. When President Burwell, Provost Wilkins, and Deans Jayaswal, Hopson, and Campbell contacted me, they asked if I could write something to inspire their students to find their passion, to unleash their potential, to soar above their wildest dreams. Tall order.

What you're about to read is based on that speech, is a story about embracing the NOs in life, is a testimony on finding your YES. I share my writerly journey—from paying friends to come to my first book signing in 1994 (they were starving artists like me, so I borrowed money from my mother and gave each one $10 to buy a copy of my book at the event) to being a #1 *New York Times* bestselling author—in hopes that it will offer some insight into your own journey. Let's fly!

Say Yes

To dream a world
don't just watch the sky, soar
say yes to your wings.
Close your eyes,
open the window
of your mind.
Be a silver eagle
chasing the sun
with bold vision.
See a dazzling new horizon
of possibility
and promise . . .

There is a particular African American Baptist sermon which is known as the most demanding speech to deliver. Most preachers won't even attempt it until they are well advanced in their ministry. It is called "The Eagle Stirreth Her Nest," and it is about the eagle teaching her offspring to fly: how the divine can teach humanity to soar.

The lesson I've learned over and over in my professional journey, this message I'm sharing with you I hope offers some insight into how to open the window of your mind, how to have a vision, and how to see it through. I come to stir the nest, eagles. Y'all ready to fly?

Most accomplished life coaches, motivational speakers, and wealthy human beings will tell you what really matters is empathy, kindness, and love, and that you should not be concerned with chasing the dollar. Mind you, most of those folks have built their wealth, and now they are champions of hope and heart. Okay, I get it. We want better for you than we had ourselves. We've learned a little bit—enough to wish we could turn back the clock and follow our own advice. Here's mine: Go out in the world and make your money . . . Just don't let the money make you. It is okay to practice your passion *and* get paid.

You see, while I always found the quote by English poet Robert Graves "There's no money in poetry, but there's no poetry in money, either," to be quite funny (and somewhat true), I never thought it applied to me.

Being a poet, I have often been scolded for holding two seemingly opposing forces at once: business and art. But I am here to tell you that we often have to hold conflicting realities at one time, and that ultimately, if we can do this in other parts of our life, we become more open-minded people. Being able to see more than one point of view is essential to changing the world positively.

I want to share a story about being bold and chasing possibility, and that story begins with one word.

Researchers have confirmed that language has the power to make the invisible appear real. Scientists believe that a single word can alter perceptions. And that word is YES.

This is what I know: When you say YES to yourself, you are allowing your own words to shape your perception. You are saying, I allow me to shape my reality instead of having it shaped for me by others. I am a "Say YES" person. I *love* saying YES. Now, of course that can backfire, like when your twelve-year-old asks if she can watch a mature adult television series or your fifteen-year-old wants to start dating.

Still, to me, YES is the most beautiful-sounding word. But it can also be a hard one to say, especially when you don't know what that YES will ultimately bring.

Many seasons ago, as a graduating senior at Virginia Tech, I participated in anti-apartheid rallies on campus. I made signs. I marched.

And I wrote. In protest, I wrote poems and produced short plays about the matter.

And I found my voice. And it felt good. So, I wrote more poems and short plays. And, one evening, the spirit moved me to write a full-length play about the harm brought by disunity and the value of community, and I believed that this play could offer something meaningful to the conversation, so I said YES to my myself, to stirring the nest.

I wrote a grant and used my scholarship money to rent a two-thousand-seat theater and staged my first full-length production. On opening night, my mother and father and wife came . . . and that was it. Three people in a two-thousand-seat theater.

Oh, it was painful. I didn't understand. I had said YES to myself. To possibility. I designed the costumes, the set, directed and produced the play. But I'd forgotten to do one thing: to market it. To advertise. There were no promotions for the play. And so, there was no audience.

You see, the Word YES creates the perception that you can do something, but the Work creates the reality. There are no shortcuts to the new horizon. You gotta put in the work.

For most people, getting a job and going to work is the first order of business in adult life. It certainly was for me right out of college. My passion was literature, and it just so happened that my father owned a book publishing company. So, on the day after graduation, while my liberal arts–degreed friends were moving back into their parents' homes and planning to work in restaurants, I went to work for my father.

Now, mind you, his business was small, and my salary was smaller: just enough to take care of my new wife and child. We ate a lot of black beans and rice, folks. But the upside was my father was a book publisher, and I had written a book of poems, so conventional wisdom said that a + b = YES, the beginning of my writerly career.

So, one day, while stapling our book catalogs, addressing envelopes, and licking stamps, I say, "Dad, I've written a book of love poems, and I'd like us to—" and before I can even finish, he sort of laughs and says, "Man, poetry doesn't sell."

My own father's great big ol' NO just slapped me across the head. Within a month, I'd resigned, because sometimes in order to say YES to yourself, you have to say NO to someone else.

On my last official workday, I remember telling him that I was going to start my own book publishing company to publish poets. And then he did something I hadn't expected: He gave me a check for $1,700. "This is a loan," he said, emphatically. "Good luck."

This is what I know: The NOs are lessons. Are tests. Are trials. And getting to the YES oftentimes requires you to not allow yourself to be defined by those NOs. You must find the motivation to work harder, to fight through fear and opposition, for the thing that you want. And the thing I wanted was to be a writer.

So, I got a job . . . waiting tables at a restaurant, barely paying the rent with my tips. But in the morning, and on breaks, and after work, I'm writing. I said YES to myself.

I took that $1,700 loan and published my first book of love poems that I immediately began promoting because I had learned that lesson (the theater fiasco). I toured—that sounds glamorous to say when in fact I Greyhound bused, borrowed frequent flyer miles from my parents, and bummed rides across the country—and performed my poetry everywhere from Washington, DC, subway stops to California street corners.

In Los Angeles, a friend had arranged for me to sell books in the gift shop of Maranatha Community Church. I had 160 books in the trunk of a friend's car. As the sermon ended, the pastor acknowledged me and asked if I wanted to share a poem with the congregation. Now, I had spoken in church before—albeit as a twelve-year-old on Youth Sunday with my mother there to help me craft a sermon I called "You made your bed, now sleep in it"—but this Sunday recitation was going to be tricky. You see, my book was filled with love poems, some of which were very suggestive. And this was, ahem, a *church!*

Talk about holding two opposing forces at one time. But I said YES, and stood in the pulpit in front of a sea of beautiful Black women in church hats and way-too-attentive little children, and recited:

If you were a ladder
I'd climb you.
Way up to the top
And I'd find you.
If you were a doorway
I'd enter you.
If you were unhinged
I'd center you.
If you were in front
I'd behind you.
Pull out some espresso
and grind you . . .

And the whole time the entire church was silent . . .
until this woman in the back yelled out:

"Hallelujah!"

I sold all 160 books, which meant I could help
pay day care tuition for my daughter and maybe
surprise her with a visit to Chuck E. Cheese.

YES means you walk through doors even when you
may not know what's on the other side, because your
eyes are on a new horizon of possibility and promise.

And you will be rewarded for trusting your vision.

The word YES is the most powerful prayer you can make. Did you know that the word "amen" actually means "So, let it be," or . . .

YES!

Over the next decade, I became obsessed with YES. I became *Ob-YES-sed.*

Still intent on having a successful writerly career, I self-published ten books, which sounds great, and it was, but it wasn't good enough to provide for my family.

So, I worked at the Department of Housing and Urban Development, and I worked at Boeing, and I worked at Lockheed Martin, and I worked at any other company in need of an editor to proofread documents. Each job was necessary, but not very interesting. My spirit was draining. My vision was waning. I was still chasing the sun, but I could see it setting and that dazzling horizon seemed to be moving further and further away. I just knew in my heart that this was the beginning of the end of my creative writerly dreams.

What I didn't know is what I want you to remember: The journey to where you are supposed to be is filled with a lot of little YESes that may be challenging and uninteresting but are prerequisites for the big YES that's coming.

As the great actor Denzel Washington told us in *The Great Debaters*, the film about the poet and educator Melvin B. Tolson, "Do what you gotta do, so you can do what you want to do."

And that is what I did: I kept saying YES to writing, even as the day slowly began to turn to night. And on one occasion, at a writer's conference, I met a publisher who said she was looking for children's books and wondered if I'd consider writing a novel . . . using poetry to tell the story . . . about a boy . . . who plays basketball.

I was not going to let this opportunity escape. She'd opened the door, a very specific door, and in that moment I thought I should walk through it, even though I didn't know what would be on the other side. And so, with my back arched and my head high, I answered YES.

I wrote every day. Five hours. For nine months. I submitted the novel to her and got a quick rejection. The poems were good, the story was weak. I rewrote the novel. In six months.

Another rejection. The story was better, but the characters weren't developed.

I rewrote it and resubmitted until finally she told me to stop sending it to her, that the novel simply wasn't working. The worst part was, I didn't know how to fix it.

So, I hired a writing coach who, for eight months, put me through a literary boot camp—redlined my manuscript, told me my crap was crap, and taught me things about storytelling that I simply didn't know.

"After reading your novel, I was left feeling unsatisfied . . . Your poetry is problematic . . . Haiku are simple, and they should always have an 'aha!' moment that surprises the reader."

Thirty pages later, I was overwhelmed with doubt and frustration, but a voice kept screaming (not whispering) in my ear, *Find your wings, Kwame . . . Be resilient . . . Chase that sun . . . All that is good and accomplished takes work . . . Put in the work . . . Say YES to yourself!*

And that's what I did. When I finished, a year later, she deemed it a masterpiece.

From there, I was referred to one of the biggest agents in the industry who promised to help me get a lucrative book deal.

My time had come. The business and art were on their way to meeting up. My creativity had a date with commerce. YES!

Weekly, my new power agent began giving me status updates on my masterpiece from publishers: Rejected. **Rejected. Rejected.**

No one wanted to publish it, he said. Not only was this damaging to my ego as an artist, but it was deadly problematic for my life, as a husband and father. You see, I'd been laid off from my job, my house was in foreclosure, and no book deal meant *no money*.

After a year and a half of trying to make ends meet,
of borrowing money from friends and family,
of nearly giving up on my writerly dreams, of
staggering in this literary limbo, I ventured to
New York to meet with him, to seek guidance, to
urgently get professional advice on next steps.

It was a lovely day, the sun shining brilliant with
possibility, when I sat down across from him in
his thirty-second-floor corner office. "So, what's
up?" I asked. "What are publishers saying about
the novel?"

"Well, Kwame," he started, "truth is, I never sent your novel out to publishers."

"What do you mean?"

"Kwame, it's poetry. As your agent, I didn't think it was a good move. It's not the kind of book you want to define your career."

There's this story about an enslaved African named Henry "Box" Brown who escaped American slavery by climbing into a crate and literally mailing himself to freedom. But here's the thing that people never talk about. What about the dude that Henry convinced to nail the crate shut after he was in it, so he wouldn't be detected? What if that guy had decided that it wasn't a good move for Henry to attempt to go postal? (*I couldn't resist.*)

This is what I know: Never let anyone lower your goals. Others' expectations of you are determined by their limitations of life. In order to soar, you gotta believe the sky is your limit. Sometimes, we need others to motivate us, to help us dream, to bounce ideas off, to rebound, to grow with. A team. A dream team. Your teammates should share your bold vision, not cloud it. So, surround yourself with people you trust with your dreams, who say YES to your soaring possibilities. (*The power agent? I fired him.*)

I grew despondent again. Lost a little more hope. Felt my wings being clipped over and over again. Over the next four years, I rewrote the book eleven times and got a new agent who submitted the book to twenty-three publishers.

I received twenty-three rejection letters. And then, on the twenty-fourth submission, I got a YES. Finally!

When this novel I called *The Crossover* hit the shelves, I hit the road, this time on a real book "tour," promoting it tirelessly in bookstores and libraries across the United States. Students, teachers, and librarians were discovering and loving it. And as the buzz grew tremendously, I could see the sun again, and it was bright.

Then it got brighter. Two decades after I'd resigned from my father's company, a year and a half after I'd been laid off from my umpteenth job, and eleven months since the book was published, I received a call that would change my life.

I was fast asleep when my phone rang at 7:16 a.m. on February 2. Startled by the Tears for Fears ringtone, I jumped up and answered it.

"Hello, I'm calling from the Newbery committee," the caller said, "to tell you" . . . I knew that the

Newbery was the biggest award in children's books, so I immediately realized this was going to be a good call . . . "I'm calling to tell you that" . . . I started thinking about all the rejections and all the NOs, and what if I had given up after the first one, or the fourth, or the eleventh, or the twenty-second . . . "to tell you that your novel *The Crossover* is the winner of the Newbery Medal for the most distinguished contribution to American literature for children."

Finally, the one BIG YES I'd been ~~waiting~~ working for. Suddenly, as the great poet Langston Hughes wrote: "Life is a big sea full of many fish. I let down my nets and pulled." And I caught everything.

The book deals came, the brand partnerships, the lucrative speaking fees. And Hollywood.

Turns out they wanted to make a TV show based on my novel. For three years, we developed and wrote and casted and produced and shot season one in New Orleans, Louisiana. And when the show debuted on Disney+ last spring, I was swimming in a sea of YES; surely there were no more NOs in my future. I had caught up with the sun, crossed over the horizon.

Life was grand, and on November 2, it got grander, when at 3:03 p.m. I received news that *The Crossover* had been nominated for two Emmy Awards: Outstanding Writing for a Young Teen Program and Outstanding Young Teen Series.

Then, at 3:33 p.m., a Disney executive called to congratulate me on the nominations, and because my life was full of YESes now, I knew he was calling to tell me we'd been given a season two green light.

"Kwame, I didn't want you to get your hopes up, so I thought I should call you now and tell you that we've decided to cancel your show. It didn't perform well, and I hope I'm not putting a damper on your spirits right now," and I didn't hear anything else he said for the next ten minutes, I just sat there feeling all the rejections. The sun was gone.

The horizon disappeared. And the hope that had been perched in my soul died.

I decided to go to the Emmys ceremony. It was a two-night affair, and on the first night, I sat in the room of 1,000 artists, entertainers, and producers, and when the Outstanding Writing for a Young Teen Program category was announced, the first of the night, I sat on the edge of my seat, wanting to win, telling myself, "I'll show those Disney folks that they made a mistake."

But the announcer called someone else's name. And I was distraught, and the only thing that mattered in this moment was another NO. Here we go again.

This is what I know: On the second night of the ceremony, I sat in the audience realizing that no matter how many YESes you manifest, the NOs keep coming, maybe to keep you honest, to keep you working, to keep you motivated. And they hurt. Hard. The NOs are a part of our lives, a *big* part. But here's the cool thing about the NOs; once they come to your party, and they get tired, and they go home, you know what's left, right?

The question is: Can you wait for the YES? Can you *work* for it?

I sat in row fifty-one of the Emmys ceremony and realized that I'd written a book that nobody wanted to publish, won a Newbery Medal, produced my first TV show, and been nominated for two Emmys, so the truth was, I'd already won.

I sat at the Westin Bonaventure and when the Outstanding Young Teen Series category was announced, I had an epiphany; as much as I knew that I was never going to let myself be defined by the NOs, getting a YES must not define me either.

Believing in yourself.

Trusting your passion.

Loving what you do is The Win.

I sat realizing that all the dedication and commitment to excellence and work that I'd put in *was* the actual reward.

And when the announcer said, "And the Emmy goes to . . . *The Crossover,*" I was already halfway down the aisle. I was already on stage, standing in front of the Academy and the thousand or so other entertainers, and my peers, and would you believe this poet was speechless. I have no idea what I said, but what I wished I would have thought to say is what I leave you with:

Be tenacious
Believe in yourself even when it seems that no one else does.

Find your voice
Lift it for the things that matter
for the voiceless
for the invisible

Stir the nest, eagles
Aim for the sky
Surround yourself with people who help you soar

Chase the sun
with bold vision

Embrace the NOs
and the promise
it masks.

Practice.
Face defeat.

Trust your passion
Be a dreamworker

Be a pocketful of plans
Be prepared for some to fail
Be okay with that

Be patient
Be resilient

Be your truth
Be grateful
for how far you've come today

for this new place you are headed
and what a delight it will be
when you turn the key
and walk through that door tomorrow
to discover all the change
wanting to be made
waiting for you to make

Be ready
to fall in love
with the world

and say yes
and say yes
and say yes

to becoming
yourself.

Epilogue

I've been told NO a lot (like you have, probably). And the truth is, even after selling a lot of books, winning a plethora of awards, and achieving prominence in my field, I still have to contend with being told NO. And it still sucks. Case in point:

Between 2014 and 2017, I performed at more than 1,000 schools, libraries, conferences, and festivals throughout the world. Now, I know it may seem odd for an author to describe his presentation as a performance, but that's exactly what it was. Along with my best friend and singer-guitarist,

Randy Preston, I took to the stage of classrooms, bookstores, and theaters—from Philadelphia to Paris, from Memphis to Milan, from Garden City to Ghana—and put on a one-man show. An hour of poetry, storytelling, trivia, and live music. I called it a literary concert.

And I gotta tell you that I felt like Beyoncé when we pulled into Castleton Elementary in upstate New York and every one of their 700 students, faculty, and staff lined the streets in front of the school, chanting my name and holding signs with "WE LOVE KWAME" and "KWAME 4 PRESIDENT."

I'd be fronting if I said that being called a "Kid-Lit Rock Star" by the *Houston Chronicle* made me feel sheepish. It didn't. In fact, it galvanized me. I kinda dug feeling like I was a bookish Bono or a writerly Wu-Tang, taking rhythms and sounds from the page to the stage. It gave me even more cred to fulfill my mission: to entertain, engage, and inspire young readers through language and literature. To change the world one word at a time.

After selling hundreds of thousands of books and speaking to thousands of students, I dreamed up a way to reach even more young readers in more places and sell even more books: I would travel the country in a tour bus wrapped in all things Kwame—book covers, photographs, cool taglines, and quotes. I'd seen other authors—Jeff Kinney (*Diary of a Wimpy Kid*), John Green (*The Fault in Our Stars*), and Rachel Renée Russell (*Dork Diaries*)—have great success touring the country in a branded tour bus. Each of them has sold hundreds of millions of books. Now, I know the tour bus isn't the main reason why they've sold hundreds of millions of books, but it certainly adds fuel to the *fire* that is their success.

I wanted that for my career, and for several years, I repeatedly asked my publisher to make this happen. "Look, it's a highly visible mobile platform that will showcase my brand, and allows for gargantuan-level exposure for my books," I told them. Each time I was met with pushback— too costly, and there's no guarantee that will get a return on the investment. Didn't faze me, though.

I just kept asking, and in 2018, they finally
acquiesced. YES!

That spring, I toured—with literary swag, a band,
and an ocean of book love—on the East Coast,
South, Midwest, and ended on the West Coast. I
was scheduled to appear at the *Los Angeles Times*
Festival of Books, which regularly attracted 150,000
readers. This was a prime location to park the bus.
All of these readers would see my book covers
and face plastered on the sides of the bus; we'd do

giveaways and make a huge marketing splash. It made perfect sense. To me.

"We don't think the festival lets buses on the grounds," my publisher told me. It was the "We don't think" part that made me question if they'd even contacted the festival. So, I called the festival offices to inquire, and sure enough, was told "You can't park the bus here." This didn't make sense to me for a number of reasons.

One, I'd seen Jeff Kinney's bus, swarming with rabid kid readers, parked there in previous years. Two, I'd seen the C-SPAN2 *Book TV* bus at the festival the year before—giving away swag bags, letting people tour the bus, etc. And three, *I was Kwame Alexander*, award-winning #1 *New York Times* bestselling author. How could anyone tell me NO?

We arrived at the festival on a Saturday morning—the largest attendance day—and I instructed my assistant Kadijah to ask the driver to pull up to the entrance gate for the festival. I tried to assuage her look of confusion—we'd been told to park the bus on a side street and walk to the festival—with my own look of, "Trust me, we got this!"

I got off the bus and approached the security guard, explained who I was, and then I went into my spiel:

"Books are amusement parks and sometimes we gotta let the kids choose the ride. This here tour bus is my ride, and I want to encourage all these thousands of kids to enjoy reading like I do.

They need to know that books are cool, and I'm the guy to do that. Would you allow us to drive the bus into the festival and park it near all the activity, so we can do some giveaways and promote my books, please?" He only offered a one-word answer:

YES!

The gate opened, we drove in and parked the bus at the *Los Angeles Times* Festival of Books, and everything I dreamed and said would happen happened: Kids swarmed the bus, book sales soared, and you couldn't have paid for the tons of media exposure it generated for me and my books.

This is what I know, folks: We're all going to be told NO. It is the way the universe works. You're going to be driving toward your destiny, and someone's going to tell you that you can't park there. But you don't have to accept it. Park the bus where you want. Get permission from the security guard first, though. And, most of all, give yourself permission to . . .

Say Yes

Kwame Alexander is a poet, educator, Emmy®
Award–winning producer, and #1 *New York
Times* bestselling author of 42 books, including
Why Fathers Cry at Night, *An American Story*,
The Door of No Return, *Becoming Muhammad
Ali* (co-authored with James Patterson), and *The
Undefeated*, the National Book Award nominee,
Newbery Honor, and Caldecott Medal–winning
picture book illustrated by Kadir Nelson.

Kwame is also the executive producer of an
animated PBS show based on his beloved children's
book *Acoustic Rooster*, and the executive producer
and writer of the Emmy Award–winning series *The*

Crossover, based on his Newbery Medal–winning novel of the same name, which premiered on Disney+ in April 2023.

Recently appointed as the Michael I. Rudell Artistic Director of Literary Arts for Chautauqua Literary Arts, he regularly shares his passion for literacy, books, and the craft of writing around the world at events like the Edinburgh Book Festival, Aspen Ideas, and the Global Literacy Symposium in West Africa, where he opened the Barbara E. Alexander Memorial Library and Health Clinic in Ghana. His mission is to change the world, one word at a time.

Visit him at kwamealexander.com.